NATURAL PHENOMENA

Meryl Pugh has a PhD in Critical and Creative Writing from the University of East Anglia and writes about interiority, environment and poetics. The author of two pamphlets — *The Bridle* (Salt Publishing, 2011) and *Relinquish* (Arrowhead, 2007) — she lives in East London and teaches creative writing and poetry for Morley College.

Natural Phenomena

Meryl Pugh

Penned in the Margins

LONDON

PUBLISHED BY PENNED IN THE MARGINS
Toynbee Studios, 28 Commercial Street, London E1 6AB
www.pennedinthemargins.co.uk

First published 2018

Printed in the United Kingdom by TJ International

ISBN
978-1-908058-50-8

CONTENTS

ACKNOWLEDGEMENTS

Thank you to Lavinia Greenlaw for her work with me on some of the poems in this collection. I wish to thank the University of East Anglia's Faculty of Arts and Humanities for the studentship which led to this collection, Denise Riley and David Nowell Smith for their work with me on its poems and ideas, Julia Webb for the sharing and talk of poems, Melanie Taylor for honouring the daily 'check-in' as we both laboured to bring our respective writing projects to fruition, and Richard Dunn for unending patience and support. Also, thanks to my *Developing Poetry* students at Morley College for the inspiring discussions.

'Walks' was commended in the 2015 Ware Open Poetry Competition. 'The Emerald City' first appeared in *The Rialto* (83), 'Although' and '3rd Person Beautiful' in *Poetry Wales* (51.3 and 52.2), 'On' in *Lighthouse* (12), '5 Delays' in *Under the Radar* (19) and 'The Pollard' in *The Bridle* (No. 13 of the Salt Modern Voices pamphlet series).

NOTES

'Green Alkanet' is after D.H. Lawrence's 'Blue Gentians'. 'Simultaneous Incessant' and 'Charentais' are after James Schuyler. '3rd Person Beautiful' is derived from a Google search using the keywords 'beautiful' and 'she'. Similarly, Googling 'ugly' provided the material for 'Ugly Questions'. 'Collapse Lament-Fantasy' owes much to the prose writings of Kathleen Jamie and Timothy Morton.

Natural Phenomena

In memory of Tara Few
1968 – 2013

Palace

Ash grotto, rain hall, fallen night labyrinth;
            demolished Palace, diminishing;
remember-ruin, ripped, defaced;
            repeat in slow motion your razed
echo. A frill, a smoke skirt, a wall
            sags, then sliding façade,
flowers in a corner: flame, wrapping a pall.
Lost turret cupola, splintering wreck proscenium,
      shattered reverb, chord fallen apart,
                        all frequencies
            flying loose, tremolo fading,
            all the burnt language degraded
      to fuzz: Palace, this your ghost,
                  your not-music.

Walks

crows hold open their beaks   heat and bleached grass

housemartins skimming their dark green reflections

nothing   no answer

*

a soft clearing   leaf sprays, squirrel-nipped

my hand on the bark: sweet chestnut in full fruit

*

dragon fly at eye level   water mint in flower
grey heron, low over the lake

marsh pennywort

*

everywhere, the wind   dogwalkers calling

to keep her
        here, fresh in the mind

    woodpecker knocking, power saw

          *

uprooted, fallen, ripped at the crown

rubble, wooden slats   tussock and peaty mud
crisp, floating bits off a bonfire
               chainsawed branches

her voice
    her way of sighing, expelling the air through her nose

        birdcalls overlapping, like trees

          *

magpies against a bone-cold sky
flat commonplace of absence

roots buckle the tarmac

    the shock preserves but then the shock subsides

hazel tassle, starling chitter, frost

*

woodpeckers, clear weather, the muddy path
again
        into a strong, straight seam of air

*

    tyres on the wet road
sun through cloud   her birthday month

a door opens and shuts on a child singing
      ladder rattle   bluebell

*

dislodged petal   wood pigeon
feeding on leaf buds

                    wing clap, arc

white-tailed bumblebee

*

thin fox ahead   a cry forced out
    no wind, no answer

*

grasshoppers, loud in the stems, the feathery tips   hips
    on a wild rose

            peacock, brimstone, gatekeeper, small copper

    swifts against a thundercloud
        the tower blocks' regard

*

quiet bird, sharp wings, thin tail
        steering, fast

this hammer, tapping
        lone sound in a quarry

Berg

This wall tower, this shut face,
this absolute rebuttal to 'city'; does it not stir
a fish flick, bear paw, cut and fin?
To press against the deck rail,
to want blue-green, deep in the mass,
is to find calling shaken out:
black tatters from a broken wing.
Powder stack, compacted crystal repetitions;
even this call scuds away, is ash scurf on meltwater,
krill for petrels, the wake of a ship — mostly prow, for
                    searching.

Although

there's no telling, no hearing and that's not the point
which I know, even when turning towards the clothes horse in
front
of the cupboard (sometimes it's you, white arms by your sides);

although it's obvious why things get lost (house keys, pens,
my glasses, my socks), that patience is owed until they're tossed
back from the ether at the whim of the Emperor of Voids;

although there are no more plans to tear down the bookshelves,
set fire to the room, torch the park, the wood, torch the whole
fucking city — no more motherless daughters or daughterless
mothers,

instead just concrete unending, or stumps, barbed wire, ruin
or annul the whole lot in one clean, decisive, hydrogen pop:
there, gone, no more to trouble us all —

although, weathered grey, I walk in my clothes and smile
and can name you in public as if in passing, enough.

Every day nothing, no answer; a lack which has made itself
at home in this room, in the park, sick of whispers. That's
enough, dear lost, dear gone, enough, we surpass you —

one birthday, another — and still the grit on my hands
in the rain, still the plaque by the tree; you persist, you are void
and the void persists although it is never enough.

5 Nights

Meniscus in the glass, agitating
shiny pinballs of talk.

Radio station, warm in the ears, cream tiles,
blue-lit underpass.

Softness falling, house of pale wings, chrome bowls
float, a flare, awake.

Fuzz orange, muck silver, an overheated hutch:
someone whispers. No one.

The last seat of the last carriage, station
lights, track dwindling.

The Landfill Oracle

They are not levelled absolutely flat, these plains
where neither salvage nor growth is possible.
Tractors promenade the shallow valleys
and bring their pincers down upon the contours:
glinting splinters, shreds of wire, fluorescent tubes,
car batteries, multitudes of gnawed bones and matter —
how else to describe it? — congealed in greys and browns.

This is a surface that is barely stable. Fresh mounds
accrue each day, disgorged by trucks, picked-at
by gulls that rise and settle with each new fall.
You might mistake them for the plastic bags
that parachute the thermals up the cliff
to catch on fences, join the bushes' rippling crops.

The day we are as distant as the gods
our children will hang over the edge of sites like this
as — like the gods — we rise in odours and seepages.
What do we tell them now, with everything

still so quick, so abundant? None of us
are able to glean what will most be needed
nor even what is guaranteed to remain.

The Lift

There are no echoes, just the pulse inside your ears,
the crackle as you swallow, leaning against the rail,
catching the smell of those who've gone before:
perfume, something fried. Like them, you wait
for your reflection to split when you arrive.

It apes a room, you think. It is not a room. A room
would never reach inside, throw down your stomach. A
    room
could not go anywhere, grant anything. Stare
into the dimness in the corners. Did you really think
there were this many floors?

The Pollard

You fell asleep, your head turned to the window,
and as you slept, that tree burst out in bud,
thrust leaves that gloved each other, flared in a rush
and stroked the window pane, then shrivelled and fell.
Whole centuries, each complicated season
played out, till the street was full of whirling leaves
but you were still closed to me.

                      I called you back —
my hand on your chest — and that bare, knuckly tree
drew in its shoots

               your eyes   strange to the room

5 Postcards

The Avenue: a double row of shrubs.
Two goshawks tumble round each other, crows
keep company with gulls around the goalposts.
Real horses pass, a vixen pelts away.

*

I thought it was a sack and brown bees hovering
but they were flies, the cat was dead, his hind legs
folded under neatly: a winter coat.
That helicopter's low, can't see it either.

*

A pit bull barrels down the bridleway
to rootle out a mangled tennis ball,
a couple of cans, an apple core, a bag
of chicken bones and nappies from the bin.

*

'Dear Bess, Just a card to tell you
Mrs C wants me to stay until Friday
so will make it about the same time Friday
evening instead of Wednesday. Much love, Lily.'

*

Against the Quakers' wall (spraypainted brick)
she looks away, his face is in her hair.
Inside the wood: a clearing, a marshy pond,
the mallard pair tucked between the rushes.

Transit

A poem for sounds & voices

soft hiss as grey enters   faint siren
as orange fades   groan in the sky
whip sound of the rails
swelling   fading   swelling   merging

Was it you I saw?

                 Was it you?

He left at eight fifteen

               No   he left
He didn't come back
I went to the station

                Railway?
Police
but we can't confirm   they said

tunnels   grown to a thunder

carriages   grown to a thunder
metal wheels   rails   carriages   thunder

Can I sit down please?
                    It wasn't my day
Can I sit down please?
                    It wasn't my day to go in
Headphones: they didn't hear
                    if I had —
release from tunnels   clanking
                    I wouldn't be   wouldn't be
groan of holding pattern
                    wouldn't be
hiss of tyres
                    it wasn't my day

That day   no one in class
They showed me the photos   after   whole
lot of them out by the statue   shouting

                    Was it you?

I opened my bag   I showed them

books   Look

                can I sit down please?

just books

What do you mean, just books?

                I saw on tv
                I didn't go in   it wasn't my day
                if I had   I wouldn't be
                wouldn't be   wouldn't be

low buzzing   rising
out of the tunnels   into the roads
down turn-offs   down High Streets
shaking the terraces into their cul-de-sacs

He whipped out his belt   yeah
come up the underpass
Fuzz in the ears
rolling it   right   and they're shouting
rolling it right round his hand
                You what? You call me
                what?

His arm

      Who did?

His arm

      Whose arm?

His arm moved so fast and

music by day music by night
the lowest growl announces the rib-cage receives
bass-line beats
filling the road cars
queue for the lights the crossing-sign
beeps like a frightened blackbird

Come to bed now it's only voices
come to bed now

      Only music

She's off in her dressing gown
sides of a tank reverberate
electric whine a tinted window

      You what?

electric window opening
bass-line drum-beat

      You knocked on the window?

They were fine about it   laughing
I see them next day   he's pushing the pram
and they wave

                   Dressing gown

it scoops you up   you are altered
set down without harm   the lights change
the traffic moves off
bass-line   receding

Her phone   right
                   Right
clamped to her ear   yeah   she said
no need to be rude
                   No need to be rude
howl of a plane adjusting its speed
the row as the carriages break into sunlight
                   A D-lock   Know what a D-lock is?
                   D-lock   Nah
Mate, breaking up
                   no D-locks here
What?
Rude?   You're rude, barging into me

                        Yeah   Piece of furniture
Like I'm a
                        I'm not a piece of furniture
Still on the other end to her mate
                        giving it all that
giving it all that
                        yeah
I said
                        Can I sit down please?

voices   the other end of the carriage
doors crashing shut   laughter

Ladies and gentlemen   there is a good
                        I didn't go in   it wasn't my day
Was it you?
                        I wouldn't be
you I saw?
                        wouldn't be   wouldn't be

clatter of carriages   faint
curl of a voice

All right?

        laughing at me: I said

Sorry   bad day

        I just

said

        make sure

make sure you're

        Sorry

Was it?

        Sorry   bad day

for years and no warning

        Bastard

        knew all about it

there you are son, push off

        till the end of the month

        and then what?

Make sure you're ok

        Was it you?

car horns   an amplified voice   many voices
the faint curl of a siren under
rails metal wheels   jolts   chains

Look   only books
and everyone looking   not looking
                        I didn't go in
Was it you?
                        it wasn't my day
Well *was* it?
                        Liverpool Street
Come to bed
                        I got off at
only the city
                        Aldgate
Car horns and a voice   many voices
faint   in gusts
                        Are they cheering?

Just voices

car backfiring   sharp against voices
in gusts   many voices   volley
of gunfire
                        Don't make me laugh
fog   voices swell   report of cannons

or guns or

                Couldn't see nothing

volley of gunfire as if down a canyon

and shouting or

                Mental

snatch of an anthem

                grit in the drink   we walked

The soot   people's faces

                Too crowded

We walked

car horns   shouting

fading

                all the way back

Faint in gusts   *a siren*

                They shut it all, you couldn't get on

slow curl of a siren

                The smoke

sirens

Was it you?

      Our faces

silence

How does a city fall silent?

whisper the rain on roads
tyres on wet roads the rain
on awnings faster on pavements
faster thunder bicycle bell faster
car horn thunder doors slamming laughter

They were all

     you know

over each other

     all over each other

three years ago Now it's all

echoes recorded voices

same station   different platforms

        over

trains gathering speed   echoes

        Come to bed

and she hasn't spoken to family for years

        Come to bed, love

        it's over, there's nothing out there

tyres on wet roads

and her Dad steps off   bottom deck of the bus

doesn't see till they're taking the corner

bell   hiss of wet road   of tyres   lurch
of a gear change   faint
sound of a train   metal wheels
on rails   jolted buffers   and the rising of blades
blades beating hard overhead   buzzing low

It was him

        No way

blades overhead
thudding and filling the ears   buzzing low
It was him   as if
he'd never got on   that day   as if

he'd just got up   stepped over the rubble
                              Twisted metal
burst free of the tunnel   as if
                              Grey
let fall the jacket   let fall the bag
                              Yellow cables   gusts
                              of ash
shirt sleeve flapping   crested the smoke   let fly   like
laughing   out past everything touched
sirens   blades overhead
                              your hands
out past everything   circling the city
sirens   the innards
of tunnels   opening wider
jet engines tearing   as faint
orange   faint grey   is clearing
yes   to blue
                              Let me see your hands
and music   bass-line   beats
circling the city   once
                              hands in the air
and voices   a tannoy   the tearing
of jets overhead

Let me see you put your hands in the air
there is laughter
cheering   hand-clapping and faint
orange   faint grey   clearing
to blue

                          Bass-line
scooped up   altered   yes   to blue

and he laughed

tearing of jets   scorching cloud
faint siren   faint whisper of traffic
quietly now:

                          and rain   and fallen roof tile
                          and mast and crane   all things
                          tending upwards
                          all things
laughed

spattering out of a grey puddle   a foot
is shaken   cycle bell
fading

                    I'm here

Was it you?

                    I'm all right   just lost
                    a heel   I know   bloody shoe

walked the whole way

                    The soot   the dust
                    my throat

Changed his name   speaks different now
                    A plumber, though?
No   it was him
                    Was it you?

Tyres in the wet   an aeroplane
banking   groaning its figure-of-eight

Was it you I saw?

Faint curl of a city   clattering hum   faint
roar of a city   faint

                    somewhere

Faintly now

                    some
where
                    you

Green Alkanet

From the hot flank of the bus to the pavement lunch
        between meetings
in the dazed, hot, infinite day of August:
green alkanet in profusion, persistent, taken for granted,
between brick wall and tarmac, on vacant sites,
untended verges.
                        The hairy, blistered leaves,
the robust, fluted stalk; green alkanet in flower stares
with clarity brewed in a white day-for-night pupil — where
        world
is altered, reversed — and holds in its blue, pitiless iris
the same blue intensity that drags us, thrashing, on —

The Talk

gridlock all afternoon   some parts of Luton
just aren't passable   not since the fens went under
and what with pirates and illegal downloads
nothing's stopping at Epping   who would any more?
boar literally   everywhere on the island

and all the mosquitos   they're picking coal off the beach
at Morecambe   there was a minke whale but it died
and when I got there   it was nothing but plastic
I had to wear carrier bags on my feet
all the furniture's gone off to the dump

the party had a crasher   did I mention the shoes?
I like a cappuccino at eleven
then I might hit the shops   you have to fight
your way through the crowds but it's worth it
wait is this the house? this isn't the house

you'd better hope no one was in at the time
don't go to hospital, no one's there   but the woman
down Hartley Road knows where to get some   I fixed
the kettle because I'm like I'M HAVING A COFFEE
and all this pale muck came out   we want all students

to feel safe   number twenty-six
got carted off last night   she never hurt no one
but that's what I'm saying   are you being torn apart?
is someone you know at risk? our lollipop lady's
a PhD aren't we all?   do you believe

in God or do you believe in shopping?   of course
when you reach that level you just don't do you?
take the next right   turn right   crossroads ahead
concealed exit   what's on the other side?
many gifts for the children we'll find out soon

3rd Person Beautiful

The woman was very beautiful, she
looked after the King. How beautiful she is.
She made pain look beautiful. She was a
beautiful person. She was a beautiful
person, inside and out. The beautiful
smile of a kind, beautiful, giggly girl.

She's definitely the most beautiful girl
here. Beautiful in blush as she
descends. What makes her feel beautiful?
If she's not beautiful on the outside, she is
not. Maybe because she's beautiful,
I don't expect her to be smart. She has a

beautiful, clear complexion. She was a
beautiful, vivacious, smiling person,
always. She was kind, selfless, beautiful
and serene. Beautiful, strong and she
used to bake. Beautiful but she is

absolutely obese. She's beautiful

and very young. She is beautiful
and I created her. I think she has a
very beautiful face. God, she is
beautiful. Lots of ways to tell a girl
that she is beautiful. How beautiful she
used to be. She could be beautiful

if only she would. I don't feel beautiful,
she said. She's beautiful. Can I say this? A
piece of ass. Yeah. Super beautiful
but she also has this charisma. She's
beautiful when she's angry. Every ~~woman~~
loves hearing that she's beautiful, but she is

beautiful, we think, bare-faced, as is.
She seems to have become more beautiful
with age. The most beautiful ~~athlete~~
in the world as she wins. Beautiful,
dynamic, she looked sixteen all ~~the~~
time always. Beautiful, isn't she?

She is a beautiful girl. She is a beautiful
girl. She is a beautiful girl. She
is a beautiful girl. She is a beautiful girl.

5 Mornings

Hooks tearing, dragging the gill against the current
or fire's sting-needle, scoring, charring, raking
or boulders jumbling, then wedged in the scoured hollows.

*

Pause at the foot of the stairs, the midpoint, the top:
no one waits with medals, congratulations.

*

In a chair on the first storey — laminate flooring,
golds and blues — while a quiet man explains.

Sash windows, crank and trundle of deliveries.
Particulate concentration per cubic metre.

*

Carbon, methane, sulphur, nitrogen —
how many elements make up a human body?

Chatting in the lift: our worried eyes
and halting, hurry-speech. *I feel better.*

*

The pillow smells of rose and unwashed hair.

Door frame creak in the sun, salbutamol sulphate,
common ragwort. Wipe down the washing line.

Ugly Questions

Do you act like a hot girl or an ugly
girl? Do ugly girls ever get any boyfriends?
Do ugly people have any value? Should you
fuck ugly girls to improve your game? Should you
keep on being with an ugly girl
when there are no alternatives? Should you
hire ugly people? Are you hot, pretty,
average or ugly? Are ugly girls easy?
Are You Ugly, Cute, Hot, Or Head Turning
Sexy? (girls Only!!!) I am an ugly girl —
does that mean I will never get lucky? I
am an ugly woman. What chance do I have? Why are
the babies in medieval art so ugly?
Why are the emojis so ugly? Why are
the British so ugly? Why do engineers
use big old ugly computers? Why do foreigners
tend to marry women that are ugly?
Why do ugly boys get gorgeous girls?
If an ugly girl marries an ugly boy,

will the children too be ugly? If your child
were to be boring, stupid, or ugly, which one
would you prefer? Why didn't evolution
get rid of ugly people? Why are ugly
paintings so expensive? Why is LA
so ugly? Why is train seat fabric so ugly?
Why is gravel ugly? Why are models
ugly? Why are feet ugly? What is an ugly
stick? What are ugly tomatoes? What is ugly
crying? Is your current PowerPoint template
ugly? How do ugly people find love?

Simultaneous Incessant

i

the faint thud felt not heard of the table's
uneven leg or a dud plug on the foot
rolled off and now, I, here, fluorescents
laminate shelving still in the eastern light
the clock face bricks red-gold the cars
and now, I, here, the desk the glass
and voices up and down the stairs crossing
siren crossing women calling there is
no car no cyclist lying on his back
across the white line and now, I,
here, fly me to the moon on piano and muted
trumpet grate of air conditioning clamped
saucepan lid van door low aeroplane
did you see what happened and I, now,
here, the pock-marked door cold peak of sweat
a pen dropped soft definite impact
of rain on grass, roofs, tarmac, fences.

ii

When I wake, it is there, already querulous and once
in a man's burr and once my own voice told me I have raspberries,
once a child called my name; a thin, high drift of question.

So loud as if we want to hear. Oh, all your notes have gone
to iron mountain, scolding as if disapproval slid out of the walls
and all this chat, this theatre of interest — no, not for me.

Collapse Lament-Fantasy

of flood and sluice-gate release; of broached culverts
and softened brick; of overspills dissolving claims;
    of such antique furred shapes down there as carpet,
sandals, greenbelt; of town clock guano stacks on lookout
    for a shoreline; of lapping tidal plastics;
of gulping beneath the ripple *all this was playing fields,*
    all this was ours; of eyot lost, no spires,
no bells announcing storm and storm, moon-pull on saline;

of planes falling; of burning petrol, of severed pipelines,
    a Chinook above a fog bank, strangely coloured;
of breathing through a rag dusts of various flavour;
    of sharing a dinghy, a wetwipe used only once;
of ill fish and only one kind; no tea to be had
    anywhere: don't climb your hill, look back
as if the sole pillar of salt, enchanted by lights
    extinguished. We're all weighed down, we're all sad.

Meanwhile: the fatberg, a supermarket sandwich; *it's*
    cheaper and quicker by car.

5 Lunchtimes

the surface as if broken
opaque as if solid

or at speed through narrow apertures
with internal shine

or to think *regal*, her tall form
a glassy upright

or extravagant volume, tumbling
bubble edges

or wind-flicked, scattered
pavement tail

Rink

The ice is fluorescent pale in the cloudy day.
Learn its ways:
the ways of its ribbed and guttery places, the long
cracks and the slight
upward curve in one corner. Practise shifting
weight from skate
to skate, using the shoulders to turn, scoring
the surface, grinding
a scouring sound from it, digging out leaves that froze
after it rained.
Inscribe what you like, or step-fall off, no one
is looking.

Mushrooms Toast Cappuccino

a man in a Fair Isle beanie discards a butt
from his open window   the traffic lights change
matching cagoules and the rolling walk of sailors
or those with sore hips want coffee eggs scrambled and toast
and tomatoes please   pinny and jeans steamer hissing
I haven't seen you   you did   did I?   yesterday
eggs on toast cup of tea

                                green beads hairband
sits upright and drinks a slow glass of water   the back
bit iffy this morning   sun   school guitar
anorak zipped right up to his neck   chews
on the toggle   his Mum come up to me then the teachers
Dad's on the phone   white coffee to go
the caff rises up   door gust   at this solo table
lime trees furling   rain and the pavement

Cicada

After the engines: the echo-less quiet of Arrivals.

Flat green, grey roads, an avenue of trees.

No shadows — no, everything a shadow.

What a conundrum, this new, sharper atmosphere.
　　It will not admit the creek, fast water over a shallow bed.
　　It will not admit the pavement, steaming after rain.
　　It rips away the shadow, moving over the cloud
　　　　under continuous blue.

A blank space, a question mark, split
　　carapace, wobbling form.

'Trick or Treat'

    floats between their masks
and the frayed rim of a paper cup:
not his mother, not her son,
not October
            or else the morning
in a house to meet, change clothes
(jeans, a hood pulled up)
                and then
a restaurant to hold a crumpled
something out on which the gaze
can't quite fasten while a phone
goes missing from a table
                or else
the man who watches from the street
making a call
          and then the holding cells,
the gates and yards, the corridors,
the trays of water beakers
              or else

van doors opening on different
landscapes, different times of day,
on pockets, shoulder bags, a language
not your own
                and if you fail,
the men who come
                        or else a pavement,
bruises, paper cup beside
this entrance to the Underground.

5 Delays

stars, pricking the air above
sheds and fences: cherry, early

lichen pebble-dashing a bridge

through the open window, a smell of hay

                    *

billboards dreaming apartment dwellers
laughing on sofas

                        mounds of brick
waterlogged operator's chair

snow, still, in long grass   the tracks

                    *

double row of poplars across
a field

     cupped-open hand — that's oak

deep-cut stream   a woman, red coat,
black umbrella   there'll be a dog

        *

new houses, pylon, yellow tractor
a loud voice: *it's a free country*

vats, pipes, gangways, gantries

                and home, when is home?

      *

smell of onions   kitchen window
then dark again

      lit clock like the moon

The Fragile

Between moored hulls that knock together,
a cormorant: diving. It surfaces, flips under,
surfaces again. The opaque water
slaps the dockside, hides the cable ends.

Meanwhile, the city wakes up: car horn, shop shutters.
The children devise their Knock-Down Ginger, their
    Bulrush.
They grin in the street at anyone. Around them
the buildings fade out, rising from shadow to nothing.

Autumn Exemplar

the chimney pots queue up for the morning   already
hauling it up   laying it out:
the thing about me is...   I felt like...

a bare shiver   a loose trail thinning

consent to be silent   preserve a quiet house
self of aura and prestige:

leaf on the precipice of yellow

1st Person

Silent, unbending, under a trickle of snow,
    I am Duchess of Malfi still
in plum velvet. I am a pale thought,
    a provisional thing, a point in the dark,
a red anorak, an old letter, toast crumbs,
    home, ever so entrapping.
What knobbly vegetable is this? My life,
    like so, arising to lean on the fence
in an overgrown garden, sit on the roof with a mug
    of wine in party clothes and a coat
in the morning, simultaneously unfolding
    rooms of music, lipstick, placards,
fridges, photos, bookshelves, receipts. I am
a dot in a city square, weirdness stripped,
    the jostle of night the window admits,
the mind which scatters and twists away and before me,
        of course, nothing.

7 Visits

a pale cave   sand   projectors

in each: the past
the images like running water on the walls

and she is here

        doesn't know why, for how long

      *

her decorated skin: clear amber lozenges
dark blue   height above

      *

outside a shop and so much younger

                faintly her
a dropped till receipt   the wind

      *

we need entrance money
she can't find the right change and we're laughing
here   I shove the silver coins at her
piecing them out of her bag

*

a long table   and at the end
amongst others

she rises: grey satin, red hair across her shoulder
giant like the goddesses and smiling

imagine if Athena heard you praying

*

a station   halls, bridges, tunnels
far down a corridor, amongst others

she is smiling, she is running

can you stay?

a marigold, between two paving slabs

just the stalk, discarded petals
orange dust around the crevice

*

I spread into sleep   accompanied by evening barbecues
the dim warm of a summer   the sun hardly behind the hills

woodsmoke   no, 'Sandalwood'

stick of incense   glimmer boundary

Charentais

It's cloudy. Tired face in the mirror: a car alarm last night.
Garlic on the fingers. Faint hammering streets away,
a metal shovel scraped over tarmac. A sparrow on the
washing line, a blue tit on the peanut feeder, wood pigeons
on the fence. The squash plant takes up half the garden,
weeds the rest. It's the first of August, summer turns its
wheel, no choice. Plane overhead. Keyboard rattle. I baked
bread, I washed some clothes, I did yoga. Rip out those
ailing roses, plant a cherry. And the day, let's hoard it, like
this melon eaten in slivers; heady elderflower, honey apple.

The Emerald City

So many purposeful rooms! Every surface a mirror:
the pink mirrors, in which we appear younger;

the grey mirrors, capturing our efficient movements;
the black mirrors, returning us to our deeper selves.

We lean on balustrades, gaze over balconies. How quaint,
our houses in the suburbs, our greyer weather. And there:

a man in a cap, shouting beside the motorway,
a woman haunting the footbridge with her carrier bags.

We too could disappear. The towers could lose us all
and still have room. We know all this.

We can't stop ourselves. We call it beautiful.

Last Visit

But the corner of four swifts' veering marks
a point one foot from the window and there's
the question of a building-height flame on Kingsway –
fire in the tunnels for cable and pipes – and so
I ask her nothing.
                  Instead, we lean, eye-deep
in movement, form; the bridge's wire ropes,
blue lights, steel pans, the prams and plastic glasses,
the ochre water that peaks and slops between
the columns tagged by Kofe and that tight swoop
across the sky, its slapdash stitching.

On

    -to the flat bed of an empty trailer sliding past
to slip through maryland   through forest gate
the yellow metal lantern   the last red light
closing the door   through ilford   through seven kings
through goodmayes   chadwell heath   through romford
toughened corrugate   load unknown   thread
drawn from a scarf   through gidea park   harold wood
and on   not stopping   six lane motorway alight
blur of night field   mudflats arising   sea glint   trawler
migratory birds   tanker horizon   kelp
and knotted cord   the congress of floating cities
triton hanjin cosco maersk safmarine   open water